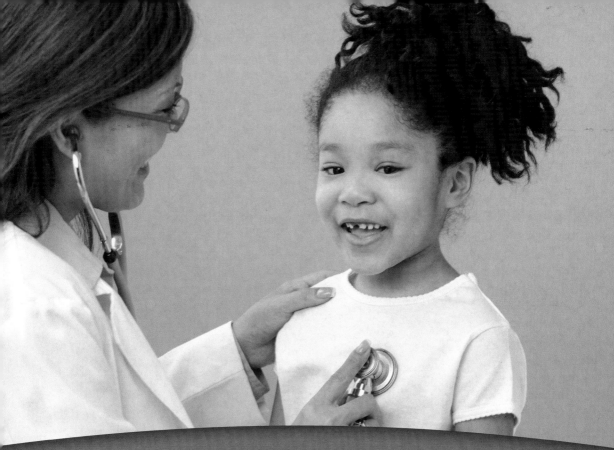

# All About Your
# HEART

## Janet Slike and Maria Koran

www.av2books.com

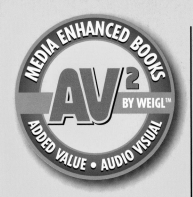

AV² provides enriched content that supplements and complements this book. Weigl's AV² books strive to create inspired learning and engage young minds in a total learning experience.

## Your AV² Media Enhanced books come alive with...

**Audio**
Listen to sections of the book read aloud.

**Key Words**
Study vocabulary, and complete a matching word activity.

Go to **www.av2books.com**, and enter this book's unique code.

**Video**
Watch informative video clips.

**Quizzes**
Test your knowledge.

## BOOK CODE

### N968928

**Embedded Weblinks**
Gain additional information for research.

**Slide Show**
View images and captions, and prepare a presentation.

**AV² by Weigl** brings you media enhanced books that support active learning.

**Try This!**
Complete activities and hands-on experiments.

**... and much, much more!**

Published by AV² by Weigl
350 5ᵗʰ Avenue, 59ᵗʰ Floor
New York, NY 10118
Website: www.av2books.com

Library of Congress Cataloging-in-Publication Data

Names: Slike, Janet, author. | Koran, Maria, author.
Title: Heart / Janet Slike and Maria Koran.
Description: New York, NY : AV2 by Weigl, [2017] | Series: All about your...
  | Includes bibliographical references and index.
Identifiers: LCCN 2016034645 (print) | LCCN 2016035183 (ebook) | ISBN
  9781489651402 (hard cover : alk. paper) | ISBN 9781489651419 (soft cover :
  alk. paper) | ISBN 9781489651426 (Multi-user ebk.)
Subjects: LCSH: Heart--Juvenile literature. | Cardiovascular system--Juvenile
  literature.
Classification: LCC QP111.6 .S56 2017 (print) | LCC QP111.6 (ebook) | DDC
  612.1/7--dc23
LC record available at https://lccn.loc.gov/2016034645

Printed in the United States of America in Brainerd, Minnesota
1 2 3 4 5 6 7 8 9 0 20 19 18 17 16

082016
210716

Project Coordinator: Piper Whelan   Art Director: Terry Paulhus

Every reasonable effort has been made to trace ownership and to obtain permission to reprint copyright material. The publishers would be pleased to have any errors or omissions brought to their attention so that they may be corrected in subsequent printings.

Weigl acknowledges Getty Images as its primary image supplier for this title.

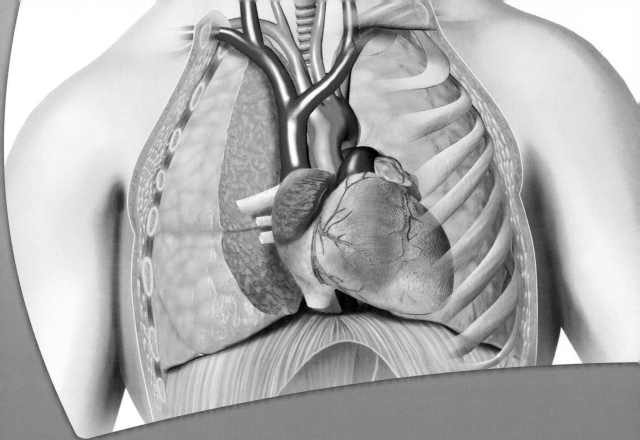

# Contents

# Chapter 1
# In a Heartbeat

Did you know you own something that pumps 2,000 gallons (7,570 liters) of fluid a day? Of course, you do not have a gas station pump in your bedroom. You have a heart in the center of your chest. Your heart is an amazing organ that pumps blood to your whole body. Blood has the **nutrients** your organs need to work.

You can feel how fast your heart is pumping blood. Place your fingers on the side of your throat just under your chin to feel your **pulse**.

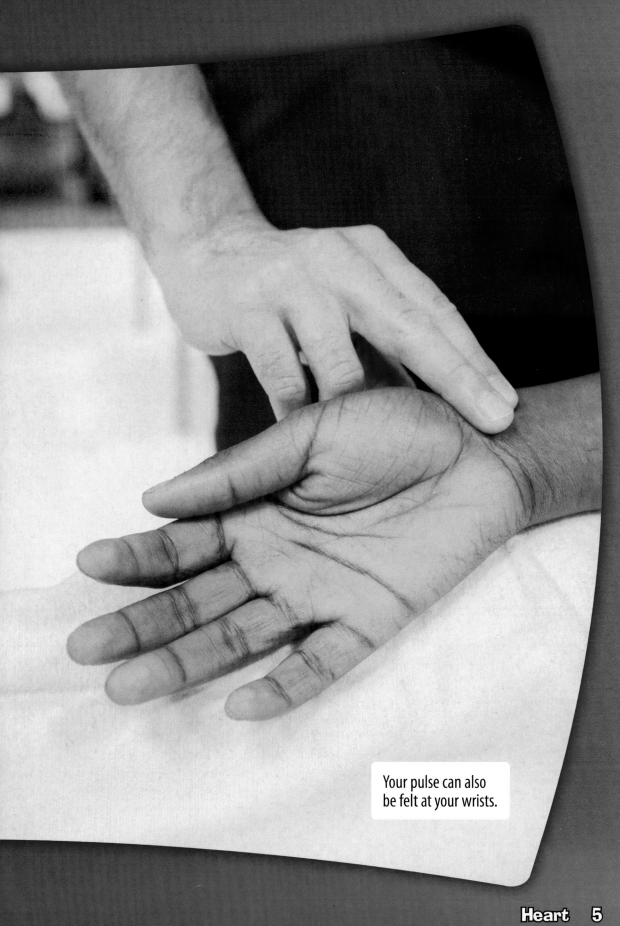

Your pulse can also be felt at your wrists.

The heart is a muscle in the **circulatory system**. It does not look like the hearts you see on a Valentine's Day card. It is shaped like a pear with tubes attached. A baby's heart is the size of his or her fist. As you grow, your heart grows, too. Your heart will always be the size of your fist.

A woman's heart weighs about 8 ounces (227 grams). A man's heart weighs about 10 ounces (283 g). The heart is small but powerful. Do you have a squirt gun? Some squirt guns can squirt water a few feet or yards. Your heart can squirt blood 30 feet (9 meters) if an **artery** is cut. This power helps blood travel through your body.

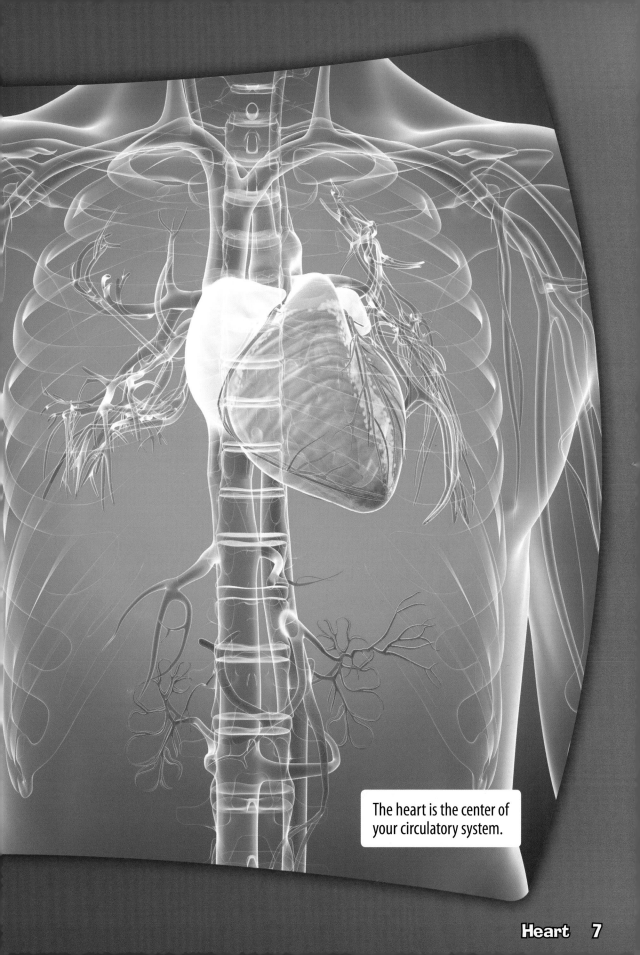

The heart is the center of your circulatory system.

# Chapter 2

# How Does the Heart Work?

The heart has four parts called chambers. The top two chambers are called atria. Each top chamber is called an **atrium**. An atrium collects blood. The two bottom chambers are called **ventricles**. A ventricle pumps blood.

The right ventricle pumps blood to the lungs. At the same time, the left ventricle pumps blood to the rest of the body. Each side picks up blood and delivers it. A single blood cell can travel through your body in 20 seconds. The right atrium collects the blood that has **carbon dioxide**. This blood does not have much oxygen. The right ventricle pumps this blood to the lungs to get oxygen.

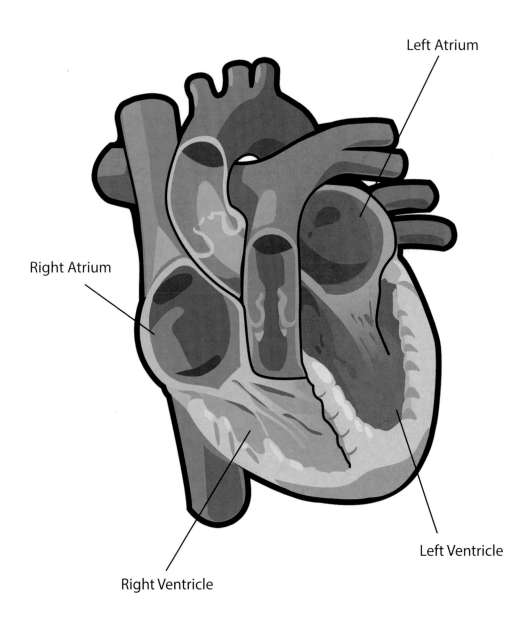

Left Atrium

Right Atrium

Right Ventricle

Left Ventricle

Blood is pumped through **veins** and arteries. Veins carry blood to the heart. Arteries carry blood away from the heart. You can remember this easily because "arteries" and "away" both start with "a." The smallest arteries are **capillaries**. One strand of human hair is ten times wider than some capillaries.

Once the arteries carry the blood to the lungs, the lungs remove the blood's carbon dioxide and waste products. Then, the lungs add oxygen to the blood. This blood goes to the left atrium, then to the left ventricle. The left ventricle pumps it out to the body. Both sides pump at the same time.

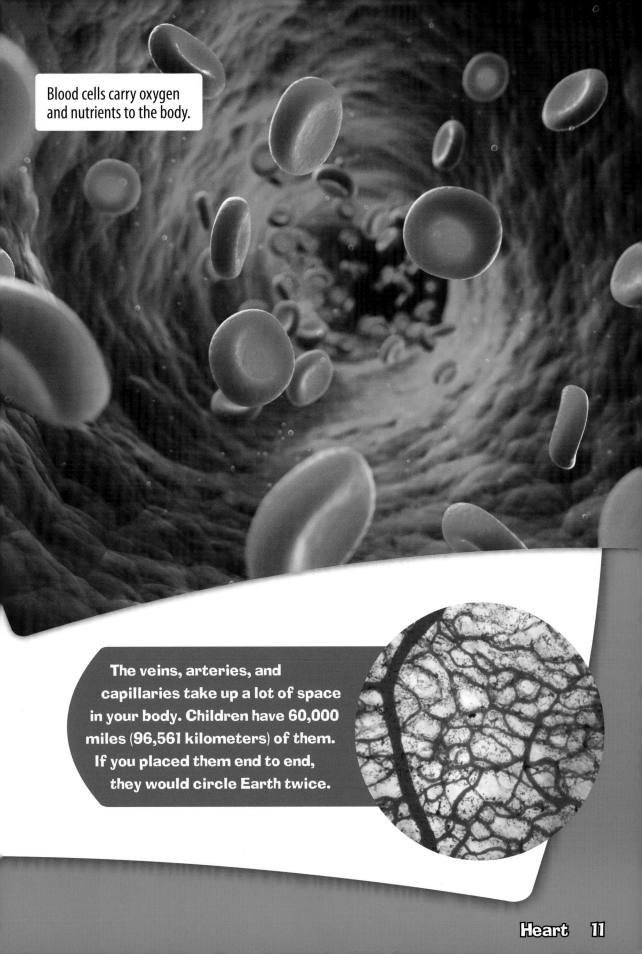

Blood cells carry oxygen and nutrients to the body.

The veins, arteries, and capillaries take up a lot of space in your body. Children have 60,000 miles (96,561 kilometers) of them. If you placed them end to end, they would circle Earth twice.

# Chapter 3

# Who Needs a Heart?

Everyone needs a heart. Long ago, people thought the heart was what made us happy or sad, but the heart plays a more important role. It keeps us alive. The heart controls blood flow. So it is very important. The heart makes sure all of your organs get the blood and oxygen they need. Without blood, organs cannot perform their jobs.

Make a fist. Open it a little. Make it again. Your heart moves like this 100,000 times a day. Your heart does not stop pumping blood when you sleep. During sleep, it slows down because your organs do not need as much oxygen.

When you run and play, your heart beats faster because your body needs more oxygen.

When organs do not get enough blood, they fail. If the brain does not get oxygen from the blood, it suffers a stroke. Some parts of the brain die during a stroke. This means the brain cannot always tell the body what to do. After a stroke, a person may have trouble walking or talking.

You cannot live without a heart, but some people live with hearts they were not born with. When a heart cannot be fixed, doctors can put in an artificial heart, or they can do a heart transplant. Dr. Christiaan Barnard did the first heart transplant in 1967.

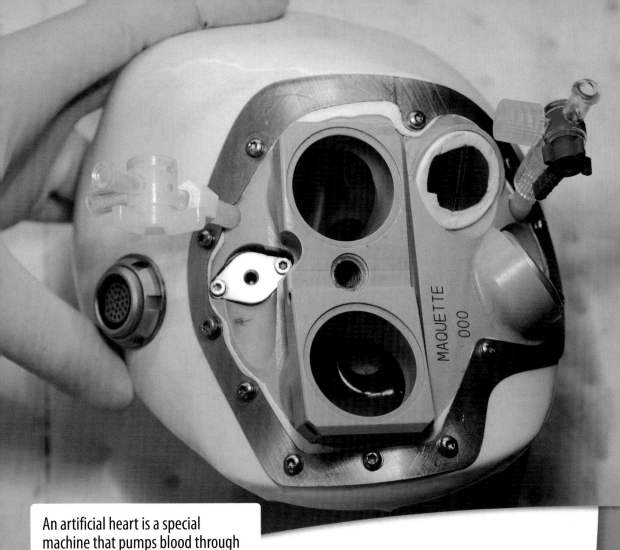

An artificial heart is a special machine that pumps blood through the body, just like a real heart.

Doctors sometimes use robots to help with heart surgeries. Doctors control the robot hands with a remote. Robot hands can make smaller and better cuts than human hands.

# Chapter 4
# Broken Hearts

Since the heart does so much work, things can sometimes go wrong. Your heart has four **valves**. Each time your heart beats, the valves open and close. They do this two at a time. The valves are like gates. They make sure blood only flows one way.

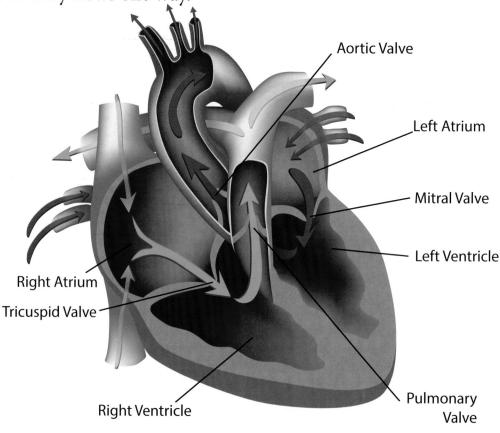

Aortic Valve

Left Atrium

Mitral Valve

Left Ventricle

Right Atrium

Tricuspid Valve

Right Ventricle

Pulmonary Valve

When a car goes the wrong way down the street, it is dangerous. Blood going the wrong way is dangerous, too. A heart murmur occurs when some blood moves backward.

An artery can get completely blocked, or clogged. If blood cannot flow through it, the person has what is called a heart attack. When a person has a heart attack, he or she must go to the hospital. Doctors can do surgery to make the blood take a different path to the heart. This is called **bypass** surgery.

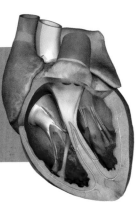

A pig valve can replace a human valve. Pig valves are similar enough to human valves to work just fine.

# Chapter 5

# Heart Healthy

**Y**ou can help keep your heart healthy. One way to help is to be active. Exercise that keeps your body moving and your heart pumping hard is the best. Exercise does not make your heart tired. It makes it stronger. Biking, running, and dancing are all good activities that exercise your heart.

The American Heart Association recommends everyone move at least 30 minutes a day, 5 days a week.

Eating a diet low in fat and high in fruits and vegetables can help prevent heart attacks and other heart problems.

What you eat affects your heart. Eat at least five servings of fruits and vegetables every day. Grains should also be eaten daily. Grains lower **cholesterol** in your blood. Your body needs cholesterol to build cell walls, digest food, and absorb vitamins. However, too much cholesterol can clog your arteries.

Foods with too much salt or fat are not good for your heart. Salty foods can raise your blood pressure. Fatty foods can raise your cholesterol and make you gain too much weight. Extra weight makes it harder for your heart to pump blood.

Stress can be dangerous for your heart. Try to not let things bother you. Do something relaxing every day. Laugh often. Laughing can keep stress levels down, which is good for your heart. So it is healthy to share jokes with your friends. Your heart works hard so every part of your body can function. Treat it well, and keep it pumping.

Remember to have fun. Enjoying life and decreasing stress can help your heart stay healthy and strong.

# Quiz

1. **Which two places can you feel your pulse?**

2. **What system is the heart the center of?**

3. **What are the top chambers of the heart called?**

4. **Which arteries are the smallest in the body?**

5. **Which part of the heart pumps blood to the lungs?**

6. **How many times does the heart pump each day?**

7. **When did the first heart transplant take place?**

8. **How many valves does the heart have?**

9. **What happens when a person has a heart attack?**

10. **Which animal's heart has valves similar to the valves in a human heart?**

**ANSWERS**

1. ON THE WRIST AND ON THE SIDE OF THE THROAT, JUST UNDER THE CHIN
2. THE CIRCULATORY SYSTEM
3. THE ATRIA
4. THE CAPILLARIES
5. THE RIGHT VENTRICLE

6. 100,000 TIMES
7. 1967
8. FOUR
9. BLOOD CANNOT FLOW THROUGH A BLOCKED ARTERY
10. PIGS

# Key Words

**artery:** one of the tubes that carries blood away from the heart

**atrium:** one of the two upper chambers of the heart

**bypass:** to take a different path

**capillaries:** very small tubes that carry blood

**carbon dioxide:** a gas made up of carbon and oxygen

**cholesterol:** a fatty substance in the blood

**circulatory system:** organs that pump blood through the body

**nutrients:** minerals or vitamins the body needs to stay strong and healthy

**pulse:** a steady throb

**valves:** the parts of the heart that control the way blood flows

**veins:** small tubes that run through the body.

**ventricles:** the two bottom chambers of the heart

# Index

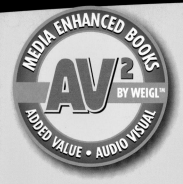

# Log on to www.av2books.com

AV[2] by Weigl brings you media enhanced books that support active learning. Go to www.av2books.com, and enter the special code found on page 2 of this book. You will gain access to enriched and enhanced content that supplements and complements this book. Content includes video, audio, weblinks, quizzes, a slide show, and activities.

## AV[2] Online Navigation

**Audio**
Listen to sections
the book read alo

**Book Pages**
AV[2] pages directly
correspond to
pages in the book.

**Video**
Watch informative
video clips.

**Key Words**
Study vocabulary, and
complete a matching
word activity.

**Embedded Weblinks**
Gain additional information
for research.

**Try This!**
Complete activities and
hands-on experiments.

**Quizzes**
Test your knowledge.

**Slide Show**
View images and captions,
and prepare a presentation.

AV[2] was built to bridge the gap between print and digital. We encourage you to tell us what you like and what you want to see in the future.

## Sign up to be an AV[2] Ambassador at www.av2books.com/ambassador.